The Life of Pythagoras

By
Porphyry

Copyright © 2021 Lamp of Trismegistus. All rights reserved. No part of this publication may be reproduced or transmitted in any form or by any means, electronic or mechanical, including photocopying, recording, or by any information storage and retrieval system, without permission in writing from Lamp of Trismegistus. Reviewers may quote brief passages.

ISBN: 978-1-63118-512-0

Esoteric Classics

Other Books in this Series and Related Titles

The Hymns of Hermes by G. R. S. Mead (978-1-63118-405-5)

The Devil in Love by Jacques Cazotte (978-1-63118-499-4)

The Golden Verses of Pythagoras: Five Translations (978-1-63118-479-6)

Gnosis of the Mind by G. R. S. Mead (978-1-63118-408-6)

The Influence of Pythagoras on Freemasonry and Other Essays (978-1-63118-404-8)

On the Cave of the Nymphs in the Odyssey by Thomas Taylor (978-1-63118-505-2)

Plato and Platonism and Related Esoteric Essays by various (978-1-63118-432-1)

Clairvoyance and Psychic Abilities by A Besant &c (978-1-63118-403-1)

A Collection of Early Writings on Astral Travel (978-1-63118-477-2)

The Smoky God or A Voyage to the Inner World by Emerson (978-1-63118-423-9)

Tao Te Ching & Commentary by Lao Tzu & C Johnston (978-1-63118-495-6)

The Magician's Heavenly Chaos by Thomas Vaughan (978-1-63118-500-7)

On the Philadelphian Gold by Philochrysus & Philadelphus (978-1-63118-511-3)

Paracelsus, the Four Elements and Their Spirits by M P Hall (978-1-63118-400-0)

Rosicrucian Rules, Secret Signs, Codes and Symbols by various (978-1-63118-488-8)

The Sepher Yetzirah and the Qabalah by M P Hall (978-1-63118-481-9)

History and Teachings of the Rosicrucians by W W Westcott &c (978-1-63118-487-1)

The Feminine Occult by various authors (978-1-63118-711-7)

The Machinery of the Mind by Dion Fortune (978-1-63118-451-2)

Brothers & Builders by Joseph Fort Newton (978-1-63118-506-9)

The Leadbeater Reader: A Selection of Occult Essays (978-1-63118-483-3)

Audio versions are also available on Audible, Amazon and Apple

Other Books in this Series and Related Titles

Alchemy in the Nineteenth Century by Helena P. Blavatsky (978-1-63118-446-8)

Atlantis, the Gods of Antiquity and the Myth of the Dying God (978–1–63118–498–7)

The Mysteries of Freemasonry & the Druids by M P Hall &c (978-1-63118-444-4)

The Rosicrucian Chemical Marriage by Christian Rosenkreuz (978-1-63118-458-1)

Aurora of the Philosophers by Paracelsus (978-1-63118-507-6)

Masonic and Rosicrucian History by M P Hall & H Voorhis (978-1-63118-486-4)

History, Analysis and Secret Tradition of the Tarot by Hall &c (978-1-63118-445-1)

The First and Second Gospels of the Infancy of Jesus Christ by Thomas and James (978-1-63118-415-4)

The Kabbalah of Masonry & Related Writings by E Levi &c (978-1-63118-453-6)

The Poem of Hashish by A Crowley & C Baudelaire (978-1-63118-484-0)

Crystal Vision Through Crystal Gazing by Frater Achad (978-1-63118-455-0)

Fortune-Telling with Dice by Astra Cielo (978-1-63118-466-6)

The Human Aura: Astral Colors and Thought Forms (978-1-63118-419-2)

A Collection of Fiction and Essays by Occult Writers on Supernatural and Metaphysical Subjects by various (978–1–63118–510–6)

Cloud Upon the Sanctuary by Waite & K Eckartshausen (978-1-63118-438-3)

The Stone of the Philosophers by A E Waite (978-1-63118-509-0)

Magical Essays and Instructions by Florence Farr (978-1-63118-418-5)

The Path of Light: A Manual of Maha-Yana Buddhism (978-1-63118-471-0)

Arcane Formulas or Mental Alchemy by W W Atkinson (978-1-63118-459-8)

The Janeites, The Man Who Would Be King and Other Stories of Freemasonry by Rudyard Kipling (978–1–63118–480–2)

Audio versions are also available on Audible, Amazon and Apple

Table of Contents

Introduction

Page 7

Illustration of Pythagoras

Page 10

The Life of Pythagoras

Page 11

Illustration of Porphyry

Page 36

INTRODUCTION

The word "esoteric" can be difficult to define. Esotericism in general can be seen less as a system of beliefs and more as a category, which encompasses numerous, different systems of beliefs. It's a bit of juxtaposition, since the word "esoteric" indicates something that few people know about, while the term itself broadly covers numerous philosophies, practices, areas of study and belief systems.

In a greater sense, Esotericism acts as a storehouse for secret knowledge, which is often considered ancient (*by tradition, if not by fact*), passed down from generation to generation, in private. At various times in history, simply possessing the knowledge of some of these subjects, was considered illegal and a jailable offence, if discovered. This usually included such general topics as Alchemy, Pharmacology, Qabalah, Hermeticism, Occultism, Ceremonial Magic, Astrology, Divination, Rosicrucianism and so on. Collectively, these areas of study were often referred to as the esoteric sciences.

Sometimes, the outer garment of a subject isn't esoteric, while what is hidden beneath it, is. As an example, Freemasonry isn't necessarily esoteric by nature (at *least not anymore*), but certain signs, passwords and handshakes given to the candidate during their initiation, are in fact, esoteric, in the sense that they are hidden from the general public.

Today, in the twenty-first century, such topics are readily available at bookstores across the country, and numerous mainsteam publishers offer beginners guides and coffee-table volumes on many of these subjects, intended for mass appeal. Books like *"The Secret"* have turned previously arcane topics into household knowledge. All that being the case, however, it isn't to say that there still aren't buried secrets to uncover, ancient wisdom being ignored and forgotten mysteries to be explored. In fact, it is often that we are only able to further our own studies by standing on the shoulders of these disappearing giants.

Lamp of Trismegistus is doing its part to help preserve humanity's esoteric history by making some of these classics available to those students who are seeking to unearth the knowledge of these ancient colossi.

So, be sure to check other titles from our *Esoteric Classics* series, as well as our *Occult Fiction*, *Theosophical Classics*, *Foundations of Freemasonry Series*, *Supernatural Fiction*, *Paranormal Research Series*, *Studies in Buddhism* and our *Christian Apocrypha Series*. You can also download the audio versions of most of these titles from Amazon, Apple or Audible, for learning on the go.

Pythagoras

THE LIFE OF PYTHAGORAS

1. Many think that Pythagoras was the son of Mnesarchus, but they differ as to the latter's race; some thinking him a Samian, while Neanthes, in the fifth book of his *Fables* states he was a Syrian, from the city of Tyre. As a famine had arisen in Samos, Mnesarchus went thither to trade, and was naturalized there. There also was born his son Pythagoras, who early manifested studiousness, but was later taken to Tyre, and there entrusted to the Chaldeans, whose doctrines he imbibed. Thence he returned to Ionia, where he first studied under the Syrian Pherecydes, then also under Hermodamas the Creophylian who at that time was an old man residing in Samos.

2. Neanthes says that others hold that his father was a Tyrrhenian, of those who inhabit Lemnos, and that while on a trading trip to Samos was there naturalized. On sailing to Italy, Mnesarchus took the youth Pythagoras with him. Just at this time this country was greatly flourishing. Neanthes adds that Pythagoras had two older brothers, Eunostus and Tyrrhenus. But Apollonius, in his book about Pythagoras, affirms that his mother was Pythais, a descendant, of Ancaeus, the founder of Samos. Apollonius adds that he was said to be the off-spring of Apollo and Pythais, on the authority of Mnesarchus; and a Samian poet sings:

> "*Pythais, of all Samians the most fair;*
> *Jove-loved Pythagoras to Phoebus bare!*"

This poet says that Pythagoras studied not only under Pherecydes and Hermodamas, but also under Anaximander.

3. The Samian Duris, in the second book of his "Hours," writes that his son was named Arimnestus, that he was the teacher of Democritus, and that on returning from banishment, he suspended a brazen tablet in the temple of Hera, a tablet two feet square, bearing this inscription:

*"Me, Arimnestus, who much learning traced,
Pythagoras's beloved son here placed."*

This tablet was removed by Simus, a musician, who claimed the canon graven thereon, and published it as his own. Seven arts were engraved, but when Simus took away one, the others were destroyed.

4. It is said that by Theano, a Cretan, the daughter of Pythonax, he had a son, Thelauges and a daughter, Myia; to whom some add Arignota, whose Pythagorean writings are still extant. Timaeus relates that Pythagoras's daughter, while a maiden, took precedence among the maidens in Crotona, and when a wife, among married men. The Crotonians made her house a temple of Demeter, and the neighboring street they called a museum.

5. Lycus, in the fourth book of his *Histories*, noting different opinions about his country, says, "Unless you happen to know the country and the city which Pythagoras was a citizen, will remain a mere matter of conjecture. Some say he was a Samian, others, a Phliasian, others a Metapontine.

6. As to his knowledge, it is said that he learned the mathematical sciences from the Egyptians, Chaldeans and Phoenicians; for of old the Egyptians excelled, in geometry, the Phoenicians in numbers and proportions, and the Chaldeans of astronomical theorems, divine rites, and worship of the Gods; other secrets concerning the course of life he received and learned from the Magi.

7. These accomplishments are the more generally known, but the rest are less celebrated. Moreover Eudoxus, in the second book of his *Description of the Earth*, writes that Pythagoras used the greatest purity, and was shocked at all bloodshed and killing; that he not only abstained from animal food, but never in any way approached butchers or hunters. Antiphon, in his book on illustrious *Virtuous Men* praises his perseverance while he was in Egypt, saying, "Pythagoras, desiring to become acquainted with the institutions of Egyptian priests, and diligently endeavoring to participate therein, requested the Tyrant Polycrates to write to Amasis, the King of Egypt, his friend and former host, to procure him initiation. Coming to Amasis, he was given letters to the priests; of Heliopolis, who sent him on to those of Memphis, on the pretense that the were the more ancient. On the same pretense, he was sent on from Memphis to Diospolis.

8. From fear of the King the latter priests dared not make excuses; but thinking that he would desist from his purpose as result of great difficulties, enjoined on him very hard precepts, entirely different from the institutions of the Greeks. These he performed so readily that he won their admiration, and they permitted him to sacrifice to the Gods, and to acquaint himself with all their sciences, a favor theretofore never granted to a foreigner.

9. Returning to Ionia, he opened in his own country, a school, which is even now called Pythagoras's Semicircles, in which the Samians meet to deliberate about matters of common interest. Outside the city he made a cave adapted to the study of his philosophy, in which he abode day and night, discoursing with a few of his associates. He was now forty years old, says Aristoxenus. Seeing that Polycrates's government was becoming so violent that soon a free man would become a victim of his tyranny, he journeyed towards Italy.

10. Diogenes, in his treatise about the *Incredible Things Beyond Thule*, has treated Pythagoras's affairs so carefully, that I think his account should not be omitted. He says that the Tyrrhenian Mnesarchus was of the race of the inhabitants of Lemnos, Imbros and Scyros and that he departed thence to visit many cities and various lands. During his journeys he found an infant lying under a large, tall poplar tree. On approaching, he observed it lay on its back, looking steadily without winking at the sun. In its mouth was a little slender reed, like a pipe; through which the child was being nourished by the dew-drops that distilled from the tree. This great wonder prevailed upon him to take the child, believing it to be of a divine origin. The child was fostered by a native of that country, named Androcles, who later on adopted him, and entrusted to him the management of affairs. On becoming wealthy, Mnesarchus educated the boy, naming him Astrasus, and rearing him with his own three sons, Eunestus, Tyrrhenus, and Pythagoras; which boy, as I have said, Androcles adopted.

11. He sent the boy to a lute-player, a wrestler and a painter. Later he sent him to Anaximander at Miletus, to learn geometry and astronomy. Then Pythagoras visited the Egyptians, the Arabians, the Chaldeans and the Hebrews, from whom he acquired expertery in the interpretation of dreams, and he was the first to use frankincense in the worship of divinities.

12. In Egypt he lived with the priests, and learned the language and wisdom of the Egyptians, and three kinds of letters, the epistolic, the hieroglyphic, and symbolic, whereof one imitates the common way of speaking, while the others express the sense by allegory and parable. In Arabia he conferred with the King. In Babylon he associated with the other Chaldeans, especially attaching himself to Zabratus, by whom he was purified from the pollutions of this past life, and taught the things which a virtuous man ought to be free. Likewise he heard lectures about Nature, and the principles of wholes. It was from his stay among these foreigners that Pythagoras acquired the greater part of his wisdom.

13. Astraeus was by Mnesarchus entrusted to Pythagoras, who received him, and after studying his physiognomy and the emotions of his body, instructed him. First he accurately investigated the science about the nature of man, discerning the disposition of everyone he met. None was allowed to become his friend or associate without being examined in facial expression and disposition.

14. Pythagoras had another youthful disciple from Thrace. Zamolxis was he named because he was born wrapped in a bear's skin, in Thracian called Zalmus. Pythagoras loved him, and instructed him in sublime speculations concerning sacred rites, and the nature of the Gods. Some say this youth was named Thales, and that the barbarians worshipped him as Hercules.

15. Dionysiphanes says that he was a servant of Pythagoras, who fell into the hands of thieves and by them was branded. Then when Pythagoras was persecuted and banished, (he followed him) binding up his forehead on account of the scars. Others say that, the name Zamolxis signifies a stranger or foreigner. Pherecydes, in Delos fell sick; and Pythagoras attended him until he died, and performed his funeral rites. Pythagoras then, longing to be with Hermodamas the Creophylian, returned to Samos. After enjoying his society, Pythagoras trained the Samian athlete Eurymenes, who though he was of small stature, conquered at Olympia through his surpassing knowledge of Pythagoras' wisdom. While according to ancient custom the other athletes fed on cheese and figs, Eurymenes, by the advice of Pythagoras, fed daily on flesh, which endued his body with great strength. Pythagoras imbued him with his wisdom, exhorting him to go into the struggle, not for the sake of victory, but the exercise; that he should gain by the training, avoiding the envy resulting from victory. For the victors, are not always pure, though decked with leafy crowns.

16. Later, when the Samians were oppressed with the tyranny of Polycrates, Pythagoras saw that life in such a state was unsuitable for a philosopher, and so planned to travel to Italy. At Delphi he inscribed an elegy on the tomb of Apollo, declaring that Apollo was the son of Silenus, but was slain by Pytho, and buried in the place called Triops, so named from the local mourning for Apollo by the three daughters of Triopas.

17. Going to Crete, Pythagoras besought initiation from the priests of Morgos, one of the Idaean Dactyli, by whom he was purified with the meteoritic thunder-stone. In the morning he lay stretched upon his face by the seaside; at night, he lay beside a river, crowned with a black lamb's woolen wreath. Descending into the Idaean cave, wrapped in black wool, he stayed there twenty-seven days, according to custom; he sacrificed to Zeus, and saw the throne which there is yearly made for him. On Zeus's tomb, Pythagoras inscribed an epigram, "Pythagoras to Zeus," which begins: "Zeus deceased here lies, whom men call Jove."

18. When he reached Italy he stopped at Crotona. His presence was that of a free man, tall, graceful in speech and gesture, and in all things else. Dicaearchus relates that the arrival of this great traveler, endowed with all the advantages of nature, and prosperously guided by fortune, produced on the Crotonians so great an impression, that he won the esteem of the elder magistrates, by his many and excellent discourses. They ordered him to exhort the young men, and then to the boys who flocked out of the school to hear him; and lastly to the women, who came together on purpose.

19. Through this he achieved great reputation, he drew great audiences from the city, not only of men, but also of women, among whom was a specially illustrious person named Theano. He also drew audiences from among the neighboring barbarians, among whom were magnates and kings. What he told his audiences cannot be said with certainty, for he enjoined silence upon his hearers. But the following is a matter of general information. He taught that the soul was immortal and that after death it transmigrated into other animated bodies. After certain specified periods, the same events occur again; that nothing was entirely new; that all animated beings were kin, and should be considered as belonging to one great family. Pythagoras was the first one to introduce these teachings into Greece.

20. His speech was so persuasive that, according to Nicomachus, in one address made on first landing in Italy he made more than two thousand adherents. Out of desire to live with him, [.........] , to which both women and built a large auditorium, to which both women and boys were admitted. (Foreign visitors were so many that) they built whole cities, settling that whole region of Italy now known as Magna Grecia. His ordinances and laws were by them received as divine precepts, and without them would do nothing. Indeed they ranked him among the divinities. They held all property in common. They ranked him among the divinities, and whenever they communicated to each other some choice bit of his philosophy, from which physical truths could always be deduced, they would swear by the *Tetractys*, adjuring Pythagoras as a divine witness, in the words.

"*I call to witness him who to our souls expressed The Tetractys, eternal Nature's fountain-spring.*"

21. During his travels in Italy and Sicily he founded various cities subjected one to another, both of long standing, and recently. By his disciples, some of whom were found in every city, he infused into them an aspiration for liberty; thus restoring to freedom Crotona, Sybaris, Catana, Rhegium, Himera, Agrigentum, Tauromenium, and others, on whom he imposed laws through Charondas the Catanean, and Zaleucus the Locrian, which resulted in a long era of good government, emulated by all their neighbors. Simichus the tyrant of the Centorupini, on hearing Pythagoras's discourse, abdicated his rule and divided his property between his sister and the citizens.

22. According to Aristoxenus, some Lucanians, Messapians, Picentinians and Romans came to him. He rooted out all dissensions, not only among his disciples and their successors, for many ages, but among all the cities of Italy and Sicily, both internally and externally. He was continuously harping on the maxim, "We ought, to the best of our ability avoid, and even with fire and sword extirpate from the body, sickness; from the soul, ignorance; from the belly, luxury; from a city, sedition; from a family, discord; and from all things excess."

23. If we may credit what ancient and trustworthy writers have related of him, he exerted an influence even over irrational animals. The Daunian bear, who had committed extensive depredations in the neighborhood, he seized; and after having patted her for awhile, and given her barley and fruits, he made her swear never again to touch a living creature, and then released her. She immediately hid herself in the woods and the hills, and from that time on never attacked any irrational animal.

24. At Tarentum, in a pasture, seeing an ox [reaping] beans, he went to the herdsman, and advised him to tell the ox to abstain from beans. The countryman mocked him, proclaiming his ignorance of the ox-language. So Pythagoras himself went and whispered in the ox's ear. Not only did the bovine at once desist from his diet of beans, but would never touch any thenceforward, though he survived many years near Hera's temple at Tarentum, until very old; being called the sacred ox, and eating any food given him.

25. While at the Olympic games, he was discoursing with his friends about auguries, omens, and divine signs, and how men of true piety do receive messages from the Gods. Flying over his head was an eagle, who stopped, and came down to Pythagoras. After stroking her awhile, he released her. Meeting with some fishermen who were drawing in their nets heavily laden with fishes from the deep, he predicted the exact number of fish they had caught. The fishermen said that if his estimate was accurate they would do whatever he commanded. They counted them accurately, and found the number correct. He then bade them return the fish alive into the sea; and, what is more wonderful, not one of them died, although they had been out of the water a considerable time. He paid them and left.

26. Many of his associates he reminded of the lives lived by their souls before it was bound to the body, and by irrefutable arguments demonstrated that he had bean Euphorbus, the son of Panthus. He specially praised the following verses about himself, and sang them to the lyre most elegantly:

"*The shining circlets of his golden hair;*
Which even the Graces might be proud to wear,
Instarred with gems and gold, bestrew the shore,
With dust dishonored, and deformed with gore.

As the young olive, in some sylvan scene,
Crowned by fresh fountains with celestial green,
Lifts the gay head, in snowy flowerets fair,
And plays and dances to the gentle air,
When lo, a whirlwind from high heaven invades,
The tender plant, and withers all its shades;
It lies uprooted from its genial head,
A lovely ruin now defaced and dead.
Thus young, thus beautiful, Euphorbus lay,
While the fierce Spartan tore his arms away."

(Pope, Homer's Iliad, Book 17).

27. The stories about the shield of this Phrygian Euphorbus being at Mycenae dedicated to Argive Hera, along with other Trojan spoils, shall here be omitted as being of too popular a nature. It is said that the river Caicasus, while he with many of his associates was passing over it, spoke to him very clearly, "Hail, Pythagoras!" Almost unanimous is the report that on one and the same day he was present at Metapontum in Italy, and at Tauromenium in Sicily, in each place conversing with his friends, though the places are separated by many miles, both at sea and land, demanding many days' journey.

28. It is well known that he showed his golden thigh to Abaris the Hyperborean, to confirm him in the opinion that he was the Hyperborean Apollo, whose priest Abaris was. A ship was coming into the harbor, and his friends expressed the wish to own the goods it contained. "Then," said Pythagoras, "you would own a corpse!" On the ship's arrival, this was found to be the true state of affairs. Of Pythagoras many other more wonderful and divine things are persistently and unanimously related, so that we have no hesitation in saying never was more attributed to any man, nor was any more eminent.

29. Verified predictions of earthquakes are handed down, also that he immediately chased a pestilence, suppressed violent winds and hail, calmed storms both on rivers and on seas, for the comfort and safe passage of his friends. As their poems attest, the like was often performed by Empedocles, Epimenides and Abaris, who had learned the art of doing these things from him. Empedocles, indeed, was surnamed Alexanemos, as the chaser of winds; Epimenides, Cathartes, the lustrator. Abaris was called Aethrobates, the walker in air; for he was carried in the air on an arrow of the Hyperborean Apollo, over rivers, seas and inaccessible places. It is believed that this was the method employed by Pythagoras when on the same day he discoursed with his friends at Metapontum and Tauromenium.

30. He soothed the passions of the soul and body by rhythms, songs and incantations. These he adapted and applied to his friends. He himself could hear the harmony of the Universe, and understood the universal music of the spheres, and of the stars which move in concert with them, and which we cannot hear because of the limitations of our weak nature. This is testified to by these characteristic verses of Empedocles:

> "*Amongst these was one in things sublimest skilled,*
> *His mind with all the wealth of learning filled,*
> *Whatever sages did invent, he sought;*
> *And whilst his thoughts were on this work intent,*
> *All things existent, easily he viewed,*
> *Through ten or twenty ages making search.*"

31. Indicating by *sublimest things*, and, he *surveyed all existent things*, and *the wealth of the mind*, and the like, Pythagoras's constitution of body, mind, seeing, hearing and understanding, which was exquisite, and surpassingly accurate, Pythagoras affirmed that the nine Muses were constituted by the sounds made by the seven planets, the sphere of the fixed stars, and that which is opposed to our earth, called "anti-earth." He called *Mnemosyne*, or Memory, the composition, symphony and connexion of then all, which is eternal and unbegotten as being composed of all of them.

32. Diogenes, setting forth his daily routine of living, relates that he advised all men to avoid ambition and vain-glory, which chiefly excite envy, and to shun the presences of crowds. He himself held morning conferences at his residence, composing his soul with the music of the lute, and singing certain old paeans of Thales. He also sang verses of Homer and Hesiod, which seemed to soothe the mind. He danced certain dances which he conceived conferred on the body agility and health. Walks he took not promiscuously, but only in company of one or two companions, in temples or sacred groves, selecting the quietest and pleasantest places.

33. His friends he loved exceedingly, being the first to declare that the goods of friends are common, and that a friend was another self. While they were in good health he always conversed with them; if they were sick, he nursed them; if they were afflicted in mind, he solaced them, some by incantations and magic charms, others by music. He had prepared songs for the diseases of the body, by the singing of which he cured the sick. He had also some that caused oblivion of sorrow, mitigation of anger and destruction of lust.

34. As to food, his breakfast was chiefly of honey; at dinner he used bread made of millet, barley or herbs, raw and boiled. Only rarely did he eat the flesh of victims; nor did he take this from every part of the anatomy. When he intended to sojourn in the sanctuaries of the divinities, he would eat no more than was necessary to still hunger and thirst. To quiet hunger, he made a mixture of poppy seed and sesame, the skin of a sea-onion, well washed, till entirely drained of the outward juice; of the flower of the daffodil, and the leaves of mallows, of paste of barley and pea; taking an equal weight of which, and chopping it small, with Hymettian honey he made it into mass. Against thirst he took the seed of cucumbers, and the best dried raisins, extracting the seeds, and the flower of coriander, and the seeds of mallows, purselain, scraped cheese, meal and cream; these he made up with wild honey.

35. He claimed that this diet had, by Demeter, been taught to Hercules, when he was sent into the Libyan deserts. This preserved his body in an unchanging condition; not at one time well, and at another time sick, nor at one time fat, and at another lean. Pythagoras's countenance showed the same constancy was in his soul also. For he was neither more elated by pleasure, nor dejected by grief, and no one ever saw him either rejoicing or mourning.

36. When Pythagoras sacrificed to the Gods, he did not use offensive profusion, but offered no more than barley bread, cakes and myrrh; least of all, animals, unless perhaps cocks and pigs. When he discovered the proposition that the square on the hypotenuse of a right angled triangle was equal to the squares on the sides containing the right angle, he is said to have sacrificed an ox, although the more accurate say that this ox was made of flour.

37. His utterances were of two kinds, plain or symbolical. His teaching was twofold: of his disciples some were called Students, and others Hearers. The Students learned the fuller and more exactly elaborate reasons of science, while the Hearers heard only the chief heads of learning, without more detailed explanations.

38. He ordained that his disciples should speak well and think reverently of the Gods, muses and heroes, and likewise of parents and benefactors; that they should obey the laws; that they should not relegate the worship of the Gods to a secondary position, performing it eagerly, even at home; that to the celestial divinities they should sacrifice uncommon offerings; and ordinary ones to the inferior deities. (The world he Divided into) opposite powers; the "one" was a better *monad*, light, right, equal, stable and straight; while the "other" was an inferior *duad*, darkness, left, unequal, unstable and movable.

39. Moreover, he enjoined the following. A cultivated and fruit-bearing plant, harmless to man and beast, should be neither injured nor destroyed. A deposit of money or of teachings should be faithfully preserved by the trustee. There are three kinds of things that deserve to be pursued and acquired; honorable and virtuous things, those that conduce to

the use of life, and those that bring pleasures of the blameless, solid and grave kind, of course not the vulgar intoxicating kinds. Of pleasures there were two kinds; one that indulges the bellies and lusts by a profusion of wealth, which he compared to the murderous songs of the Sirens; the other kind consists of things honest, just, and necessary to life, which are just as sweet as the first, without being followed by repentance; and these pleasures he compared to the harmony of the Muses.

40. He advised special regard to two times; that when we go to sleep, and that when we awake. At each of these we should consider our past actions, and those that are to come. We ought to require of ourselves an account of our past deeds, while of the future we should have a providential care. Therefore he advised everybody to repeat to himself the following verses before he fell asleep:

"Nor suffer sleep to close thine eyes
Till thrice thy acts that day thou hast run o'er;
How slipt? What deeds? What duty left undone?"

On rising:

"As soon as ere thou wakest, in order lay
The actions to be done that following day"

41. Such things taught he, though advising above all things to speak the truth, for this alone deifies men. For as he had learned from the Magi, who call God Oremasdes, God's body is light, and his soul is truth. He taught much else, which he claimed to have learned from Aristoclea at Delphi. Certain things he declared mystically, symbolically, most of which were collected by Aristotle, as when he called the sea a *tear of Saturn*;

the two bear (constellations) *the hand of Rhea*; the Pleiades, *the lyre of the Muses*; the Planets, *the dogs of Persephone*; and he called be sound caused by striking on brass the voice of a genius enclosed in the brass.

42. He had also another kind of symbol, such as, pass not over a balance; that is, Shun avarice. Poke not the fire with a sword, that is, we ought not to excite a man full of fire and anger with sharp language. Pluck not a crown, meant not to violate the laws, which are the crowns of cities. Eat not the heart, signified not to afflict ourselves with sorrows. Do not sit upon a [pack]-measure, meant, do not live ignobly. On starting a journey, do not turn back, meant, that this life should not be regretted, when near the bourne of death. Do not walk in the public way, meant, to avoid the opinions of the multitude, adopting those of the learned and the few. Receive not swallows into your house, meant, not to admit under the same roof garrulous and intemperate men. Help a man to take up a burden, but not to lay it down, meant, to encourage no one to be indolent, but to apply oneself to labor and virtue. Do not carry the images of the Gods in rings, signified that one should not at once to the vulgar reveal one's opinions about the Gods, or discourse about them. Offer libations to the Gods, just to the ears of the cup, meant, that we ought to worship and celebrate the Gods with music, for that penetrates through the ears. Do not eat those things that are unlawful, sexual or increase, beginning nor end, nor the first basis of all things.

43. He taught abstention from the loins, testicle, pudenda, marrow, feet and heads of victims. The loins he called *basis*, because on them as foundations living beings are settled.

Testicles and pudenda he called *generation*, for no one is engendered without the help of these. Marrow he called *increase* as it is the cause of growth in living beings. The *beginning* was the feet, and the head the end; which have the most power in the government of the body. He likewise advised abstention from beans, as from human flesh.

44. Beans were interdicted, it is said, because the particular plants grow and individualize only after (the earth) which is the principle and origin of things, is mixed together, so that many things underground are confused, and coalesce; after which everything rots together. Then living creatures were produced together with plants, so that both men and beans arose out of putrefaction whereof he alleged many manifest arguments. For if anyone should chew a bean, and having ground it to a pulp with his teeth, and should expose that pulp to the warm sun, for a short while, and then return to it, he will perceive the scent of human blood. Moreover, if at the time when beans bloom, one should take a little of the flower, which then is black, and should put it into an earthen vessel, and cover it closely, and bury in the ground for ninety days, and at the end thereof take it up, and uncover it, instead of the bean he will find either the head of an infant, or the pudenda of a woman.

45. He also wished men to abstain from other things, such as a swine's paunch, a mullet, and a sea-fish called a "nettle," and from nearly all other marine animals. He referred his origin to those of past ages, affirming that he was first Euphorbus, then Aethalides, then Hermotimus, then Pyrrhus, and last, Pythagoras. He showed to his disciples that the soul is immortal, and to those who were rightly purified he brought back the memory of the acts of their former lives.

46. He cultivated philosophy, the scope of which is to free the mind implanted within us from the impediments and fetters within which it is confined; without whose freedom none can learn anything sound or true, or perceive the unsoundedness in the operation of sense. Pythagoras thought that mind alone sees and hears, while all the rest are blind and deaf. The purified mind should be applied to the discovery of beneficial things, which can be effected by, certain artificial ways, which by degrees induce it to the contemplation of eternal and incorporeal things, which never vary. This orderliness of perception should begin from consideration of the most minute things, lest by any change the mind should be jarred and withdraw itself, through the failure of continuousness in its subject-matter.

47. That is the reason he made so much use of the mathematical disciplines and speculations, which are intermediate between the physical and the incorporeal realm, for the reason that like bodies they have a threefold dimension, and yet share the impassibility of incorporeals; as degrees of preparation to the contemplation of the really existent things; by an artificial reason diverting the eyes of the mind from corporeal things, whose manner and state never remain in the same condition, to a desire for true (spiritual) food. By means of these mathematical sciences therefore, Pythagoras rendered men truly happy, by this artistic introduction of truly [consistent] things.

48. Among others, Moderatus of Gades, who [learnedly] treated of the qualities of numbers in seven books, states that the Pythagoreans specialized in the study of numbers to explain their teachings symbolically, as do geometricians, inasmuch as the primary forms and principles are hard to understand and express, otherwise, in plain discourse. A similar case is the representation of sounds by letters, which are known by marks, which are called the first elements of learning; later, they inform us these are not the true elements, which they only signify.

49. As the geometricians cannot express incorporeal forms in words, and have recourse to the descriptions of figures, as that is a triangle, and yet do not mean that the actually seen lines are the triangle, but only what they represent, the knowledge in the mind, so the Pythagoreans used the same objective method in respect to first reasons and forms. As these incorporeal forms and first principles could not be expressed in words, they had recourse to demonstration by numbers. Number one denoted to them the reason of Unity, Identity, Equality, the purpose of friendship, sympathy, and conservation of the Universe, which results from persistence in Sameness. For unity in the details harmonizes all the parts of a whole, as by the participation of the First Cause. .

50. Number two, or *Duad*, signifies the two-fold reason of diversity and inequality, of everything that is divisible, or mutable, existing at one time in one way, and at another time in another way. After all these methods were not confined to the Pythagoreans, being used by other philosophers to denote unitive powers, which contain all things in the universe, among which are certain reasons of equality, dissimilitude and diversity. These reasons are what they meant by the terms *Monad* and *Duad*, or by the words uniform, biform, or diversiform.

51. The same reasons apply to their use of other numbers, which were ranked according to certain powers. Things that had a beginning, middle and end, they denoted by the number Three, saying that anything that has a middle is triform, which was applied to every perfect thing. They said that if anything was perfect it would make use of this principle and be adorned, according to it; and as they had no other name for it, they invented the form *Triad*; and whenever they tried to bring us to the knowledge of what is perfect they led us to that by the form of this *Triad*. So also with the other numbers, which were ranked according to the same reasons.

52. All other things were comprehended under a single form and power which they called *Decad*, explaining it by a pun as decad, meaning comprehension. That is why they called Ten a perfect number, the most perfect of all as comprehending all difference of numbers, reasons, species and proportions. For if the nature of the universe be defined according to the reasons and proportions of members, and if that which is produced, increased and perfected, proceed according to the reason of numbers; and since the *Decad* comprehends every reason of numbers, every proportion, and every species, why should Nature herself not be denoted by the most perfect number, Ten? Such was the use of numbers among the Pythagoreans.

53. This primary philosophy of the Pythagoreans finally died out first, because it was enigmatical, and then because their commentaries were written in Doric, which dialect itself is somewhat obscure, so that Doric teachings were not fully understood, and they became misapprehended, and finally spurious, and later, they who published them no longer were Pythagoreans. The Pythagoreans affirm that Plato, Aristotle, Speusippus, Aristoxenus and Xenocrates; appropriated the best of them, making but minor changes (to distract attention from this their theft), they later collected and delivered as characteristic Pythagorean doctrines whatever therein was most trivial, and vulgar, and whatever had been invented by envious and calumnious persons, to cast contempt on Pythagoreanism.

54. Pythagoras and his associates were long held in such admiration in Italy, that many cities invited them to undertake their administration. At last, however, they incurred envy, and a conspiracy was formed against them as follows. Cylon, a Crotonian, who in race, nobility and wealth was the most preeminent, was of a severe, violent and tyrannical disposition, and did not scruple to use the multitude of his followers to compass his ends. As he esteemed himself worthy of whatever was best, he considered it his right to be admitted to Pythagorean fellowship. He therefore went to Pythagoras extolled himself, and desired his conversation. Pythagoras, however, who was accustomed to read in human bodies' nature and manners the disposition of the man, bade him depart, and go about his business. Cylon, being of a rough and violent disposition, took it as a great affront, and became furious.

55. He therefore assembled his friends, began to accuse Pythagoras, and conspired against him and his disciples. Pythagoras then went to Delos, to visit the Syrian Pherecydes, formerly his teacher, who was dangerously sick, to nurse him. Pythagoras's friends then gathered together in the house of Milo the wrestler; and were all stoned and burned when Cylo's followers set the house on fire. Only two escaped, Archippus and Lysis, according to the account of Neanthes. Lysis took refuge in Greece, with Epaminondas, whose teacher he had formerly been.

56. But Dicaearchus and other more accurate historians relate that Pythagoras himself was present when this conspiracy bore fruit, for Pherecydes had died before he left Samos. Of his friends, forty who were gathered together in a house were attacked and slain; while others were gradually slain as they came to the city. As his friends were taken, Pythagoras himself first escaped to the Caulonian haven, and thence visited the Locrians. Hearing of his coming, the Locrians sent some old men to their frontiers to intercept him. They said, "Pythagoras, you are wise and of great worth; but as our laws retain nothing reprehensible, we will preserve them intact. Go to some other place, and we will furnish you with any needed necessaries of travel." Pythagoras turned back, and sailed to Tarentum, where, receiving the same treatment as at Crotona, he went to Metapontum. Everywhere arose great mobs against him, of which even now the inhabitants make mention, calling them the Pythagorean riots, as his followers were called Pythagoreans.

57. Pythagoras fled to the temple of the Muses, in Metapontum. There he abode forty days, and starving, died. Others however state that his death was due to grief at the loss of all his friends who, when the house in which they were gathered was burned, in order to make a way for their master, they threw themselves into the flames, to make a bridge of safety for him, whereby indeed he escaped. When died the Pythagoreans, with them also died their knowledge, which till then than they had kept secret, except for a few obscure things which were commonly repeated by those who did not understand them. Pythagoras himself left no book; but some little sparks of his philosophy, obscure and difficult, were preserved by the few who were preserved by being scattered, as were Lysis and Archippus.

58. The Pythagoreans now avoided human society, being lonely, saddened and dispersed. Fearing nevertheless that among men the name of philosophy would be entirely extinguished, and that therefore the Gods would be angry with them, they made abstracts and commentaries. Each man made his own collection of written authorities and his own memories, leaving them wherever he happened to die, charging their wives, sons and daughters to preserve them within their families. This mandate of transmission within each family was obeyed for a long time.

59. Nichomacus says that this was the reason why the Pythagoreans studiously avoided friendship with strangers, preserving a constant friendship among each other. Aristoxenus, in his book on the *Life of Pythagoras*, says he heard many things from Dionysius, the tyrant of Sicily, who, after his abdication, taught letters at Corinth. Among these were that they abstained from lamentations and grieving and tears; also from adulation, entreaty, supplication and the like.

60. It is said that Dionysius at one time wanted to test their mutual fidelity under imprisonment. He contrived this plan. Phintias was arrested, and taken before the tyrant, and charged with plotting against the tyrant, convicted, and condemned to death. Phintias, accepting the situation, asked to be given the rest of the day to arrange his own affairs, and those of Damon, his friend and associate, who now would have to assume the management. He therefore asked for a temporary release, leaving Damon as security for his appearance. Dionysius granted the request, and they sent for Damon, who agreed to remain until Phintias should return.

61. The novelty of this deed astonished Dionysius; but those who had first suggested the experiment, scoffed at Damon, saying he was in danger of losing his life. But to the general surprise, near sunset Phintias came to die. Dionysius then expressed his admiration, embraced them both, and asked to be received as a third in their friendship. Though he earnestly besought this, they refused this, though assigning no reason therefore. Aristoxenus states he heard this from Dionysius himself. [Hippobotus] and Neanthes relate about Myllia and Timycha.

Porphyry

www.ingramcontent.com/pod-product-compliance
Lightning Source LLC
LaVergne TN
LVHW041503070426
835507LV00009B/784